Skateboards and Skateboarding

The Complete Beginner's Guide

Skateboards and Skateboarding

The Complete Beginner's Guide

by La Vada Weir

Photographs by AL MOOTE

Illustrations by W. E. HOPMANS

Julian Messner New York

Printed in the United States of America

Design by Marjorie Zaum

Fourth Printing, 1978

Library of Congress Cataloging in Publication Data

Weir, LaVada.
  Skateboards and skateboarding.
  SUMMARY: Skateboarding techniques and tricks with advice for buying, making, and caring for a skateboard.
  1. Skateboarding—Juvenile literature. [1. Skate-boarding] I. Moote, Al. II. Hopmans, W. E.
III. Title.
GV859.8.W44   796.2'1   76-51296
ISBN 0-671-32828X

Foreword

IN THE LAST TEN YEARS, I HAVE SEEN SKATE-
boarding develop from playing on a dangerous toy to becoming a full-fledged sport.

Kids today are dynamic, creative, and sophisticated. It makes sense that they would go for an exciting sport— a sport which could grow only because of technical improvements in the equipment. And a sport which allows each skater the opportunity to express himself or herself.

The continuing development of the sport now depends upon two things: a proper place for skateboarding, and skateboarders who can add to the growth of the sport.

In reading *Skateboards and Skateboarding:* The Complete Beginner's Guide, you will find, as I did, complete and accurate instructions on how to skateboard and to do some tricks. It will also show you how to have fun and not get hurt. You can learn how to take care of your equipment, get the best for your money, or build your own. And it's interesting to learn how skateboarding began and grew.

Jack Dimon, Skateboard Consultants
Co/Mark Communications/Marketing Group
Newport Beach, California

Contents

CHAPTER 1

How It All Began

DID YOU EVER WISH YOU HAD WINGS ON YOUR feet? That you could whiz along above the ground and never touch it? You probably have. Lots of people have—which may explain why skateboarding is so popular.

How did skateboarding get started? Who was the first skateboarder?

EARLY ANCESTOR

Back in the early 1920s, a popular toy on rubber wheels was the scooter. It had a board to stand on and a post with handles to guide with. The scooter was followed by a similar model called a skate coaster.

In the 1930s, the skate coaster was popular, too, because it was cheap to make. If you had only one good roller skate, a length of 2 by 4 wood, and another length of wood for the steering post, you could build your own skate coaster. But the envy of the neighborhood was the soapbox scooter. It was made with roller skate wheels attached to a board, and a wooden soap box or orange crate in place of the post. You

steered with the two handles on the box.

You couldn't do much on a skate coaster, except make a lot of noise. If anyone tried riding the board without its steering post, it didn't catch on. Thirty years later, it did.

SIDEWALK SURFING

It began in a little southern California beach town, where the hills run down to the Pacific Ocean. Surfboarding was a popular sport there—when the ocean wasn't too rough or too calm. It was calm one day back in the 1950s, and a surfboarder with no surf was unhappy. He had nothing to do.

Suddenly, he had an idea. He nailed old roller skate wheels to a water ski, and tried riding it downhill as he would ride his surfboard down a wave. He crashed against the pavement and came up bleeding from the scratches. (These injuries later came to be known as "road rash" with "strawberries" and "hamburgers," depending on how much skin you lost.) Practicing, he finally balanced himself on the ski and rode downhill, using surfing body movements. Sidewalk surfing was born!

That first sidewalk surfer may or may not have been the champion surfer, Hobie Alter. No one knows for sure. But Hobie does admit that in the 1950s, he fashioned special hardwood boards with skate wheels for riding the hills.

He didn't like the stiff, steel roller skate wheels. They didn't roll easily, and they slipped and slid on hard surfaces. So he experimented. He found that the "clay" wheels used on rink roller skates worked better. They didn't last long on pavement because they were made of plastic, paper, and finely ground walnut shells. But they gave a smoother ride and were somewhat easier to control in the turns.

Hobie began making boards for his friends. Soon he was manufacturing and selling *skateboards,* as they came to be called. In 1959, he toured the California beach towns demonstrating how to skateboard. Two years later, skateboarding was nationally known. And at the age of 25, Hobie Alter was the "Granddaddy of Skateboarding."

In 1963, there were half a dozen manufacturers of skate-

boards. They sponsored teams, and sent them around the country to advertise their products.

Skateboarding was becoming a national craze. Other companies and individuals began manufacturing skateboards to meet the sudden demand.

BIG BUSINESS

The 1960s were a time of business and manufacturing growth, and companies were looking for ways to become bigger. The Vita-Pak Juice Company in Covina, California, was one of these. They asked their employees for ideas.

During a weekend at the beach, Ed Morgan, a young executive in the Vita-Pak sales department, had watched the sidewalk surfers. On Monday morning, when he saw stacks of empty wooden orange crates in the Vita-Pak warehouse, he came up with an idea. Vita-Pak had just bought a nearby roller skate factory, and he got some wheels from them. Taking a slat from a crate, he rounded off one end with his pocket knife. Back in his office, he fastened some roller skate wheels onto the narrow piece of board. When he explained his idea, Vita-Pak liked it and began manufacturing skateboards.

They asked Hobie Alter for design advice, and in 1965, came out with a fiberglass skateboard called a Hobie. Vita-Pak also sponsored a team to tour the country. The team demonstrated what fun could be had on a skateboard. That year, the company had to produce 25,000 skateboards every day

to meet the demand. And 50 million were sold by all the companies manufacturing skateboards.

SKATEBOARDING OUTLAWED

But the skateboard craze didn't last.

The "clay" wheels broke up too easily. After seven or eight hours of hard, downhill skating, they were of no use. If a wheel hit a pebble on the pavement, the skateboard stopped but the skater did not.

Because of the poor wheels, skaters were limited in what they could do. Once they had mastered a few tricks and raced downhill, there was nothing more they could do. There were no more challenges.

Yet, some skaters kept trying to do more than they or their equipment could. They had more and more accidents, and they gave the sport a bad name. Orthopedists coined a new medical term, "skateboard fracture," to describe the broken bones resulting from skateboarding accidents. There were also deaths. Finally, some city agencies, the American Medical Association, and parent groups recommended that skateboards be outlawed.

Suddenly, the companies that had been manufacturing skateboards had no customers. Vita-Pak was left with four warehouses, each holding a million dollars worth of skate-

boards. It was the beginning of 1966, and skateboarding was dead.

"INVENTOR OF THE WHEEL"

In 1970, Frank Nasworthy, a surfer and skateboarder, had just graduated from high school. He left his home town of Encinitas, California, to attend the Virginia Polytechnic Institute. He wanted to become an engineer. But Frank got

16

involved with a political demonstration and was suspended from school. Before going back to California, he visited relatives in Purcellville, Virginia. They owned a small company called Creative Urethane, Inc. which manufactured *polyurethane* wheels for rink roller skates.

Because polyurethane wheels tended to grip the floor, they were slow. "Clay" wheels were much faster. But the polyurethane lasted longer, so rink owners used them on their rental skates.

Frank was interested. No doubt influenced by his memories of surf and hills back home, he saw how the wheels could be used for skateboards. When he returned to Encinitas, he took some of them with him.

At home, he figured out a way to attach the polyurethane wheels to his old skateboard and went for a ride. He found the new wheels didn't slip or slide. They held to the pavement, and ran over small rocks without stopping. Even after much riding, they showed almost no signs of wear.

Frank had saved up $700.00 from working in a restaurant. He decided to go into the business of supplying polyurethane wheels for skateboards. Now he made business arrangements with his relatives to manufacture wheels he had designed. Then he chose a name for his company. It was Cadillac Wheels Co., because he knew Cadillac cars had the reputation for a cushiony ride, for being mechanically the best, and for lasting quality. His wheels had the same features. He called himself "Captain Cadillac" and toured the country giving demonstrations. Soon skateboarders everywhere affectionately called him the "Inventor of the Wheel."

REBIRTH OF SKATEBOARDING

By 1974, skateboarding had again become a national craze. It even spread around the world so that today equipment is exported to Japan, Australia, New Zealand, South Africa, Europe, and South America.

To keep up with the skateboard craze, a magazine, *Skateboarder,* was started. Skateboarding and its champions

are the subject of television programs, educational films, and movies.

The first community skateboard park (admission is free) in the United States was built in Ventura, California. Shortly afterward, commercial parks (where they charge admission) appeared in Japan, Australia, California, Florida, and Texas. More are opening.

There are skateboard organizations which sponsor competitions for national and world titles. The first world championship competition was held in San Diego in 1975. Some of the champions have gone on to become professionals. They tour the world, demonstrating how to skateboard safely and for fun.

CHAPTER 2

What's a Skateboard?

A SKATEBOARD IS FOR HAVING FUN. BUT IF you're really going into skateboarding, you'll want to know more than that.

First of all, there are special names for the parts of a skateboard.

THE BOARD

The *board* is the body of the skateboard. It, also, has two other names, a *blank* or a *chassis* (shas'-ee). The board can be made of wood, plastic, or metal. Boards are manufactured in lengths from 19 inches to 48 inches. Widths range from 3 inches to 7 inches. The most popular size is 24 inches long by 7 inches wide.

The shorter boards are used mostly by small skate-

Wheels

Tail

Truck

Base plate

Board, Blank or Chassis

Rail

Axle

Nose

Skateboard parts. (This skateboard does not have a pad, or shock absorber, between the board and the base plate.)

boarders or for doing tricks. The longer boards are used by tall or heavy skateboarders, or for downhill skating.

The top of the board is called the *deck*. The deck is usually smooth and shiny when new. You must put on a pattern of *grip tape* (a nonskid tape such as is used on swimming pool steps) so that it won't be slippery.

The front end of the board is the *nose*. Usually the nose is rounded, or narrower than the rest of the board. The rear

21

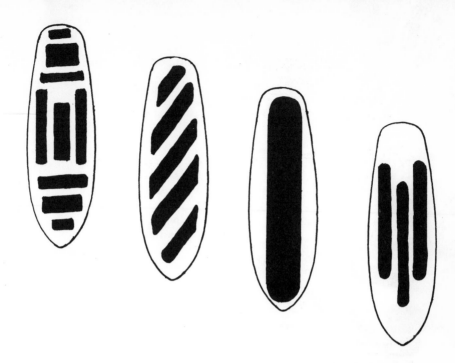

end is the *tail*. A tail that curves up is a *kicktail, or kick.*
When both the nose and the tail curve up, it is a *double-kick.*
(The use of the kick is explained in the chapter on tricks.)

TRUCKS

Near each end of the board is a metal unit, or assembly,
called a *truck* to which the wheels are attached. An axle which
is used for the wheels fits into the truck.

The most widely used truck is the *double-action adjustable* truck. It is called "double-action" because it has two
bushings, one above and one below the axle. Bushings are
made of rubber or vinyl and act as cushions, or *shock*

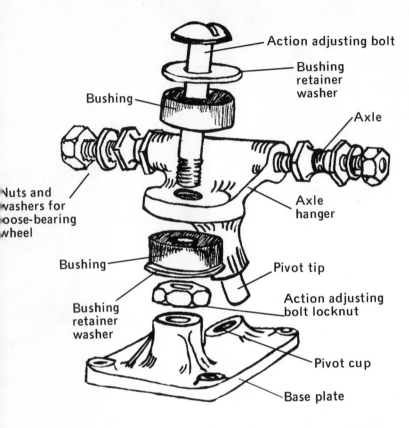

Action adjusting bolt

Bushing retainer washer

Bushing

Axle

Nuts and washers for loose-bearing wheel

Axle hanger

Bushing

Pivot tip

Bushing retainer washer

Action adjusting bolt locknut

Pivot cup

Base plate

Double-action adjustable truck for loose bearings.

absorbers. Most everyone calls them "shocks." They are also known as *kingpin spacers*.

BASE PLATE

Next to the board is the *base plate* which the truck is bolted into. A base plate is either made of metal or heavy-duty plastic.

Between the base plate and the board there may, or may

24

not be, another shock absorber. This, too, has other names—
base-plate spacer, or *pad.* It is made of rubber or vinyl to
absorb riding vibrations.

WHEELS

Wheels are made of polyurethane. Skateboarders refer
to it as *urethane.*

Polyurethane wheels look like hard candy. They can
have any color added when they are being manufactured.
Red, yellow and clear are the most popular.

Wheels come in different sizes. Smaller wheels are best

Wheel with sealed precision bearings.

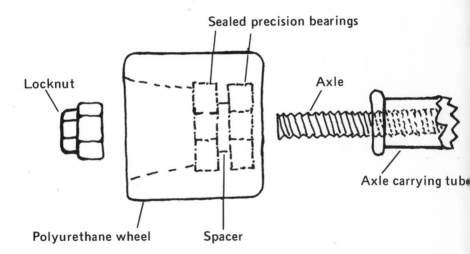

for doing tricks. They are more maneuverable. Wide wheels are for downhill racing. There is more about wheel sizes in Chapter 6.

Wheels have one of two types of bearings: either the old loose ball bearings or the new sealed precision bearings.

With the loose bearings, a bearing can pop out, causing its wheel to roll differently from the other three wheels. This can cause an accident. The bearing must be replaced with a new one. The precision bearings are sealed in and will not pop out. They roll quietly, giving you a chance to hear what may be behind you. And they give a smoother ride. But they cost more.

CHAPTER 3

Getting Ready to Skateboard

YOU CAN LEARN SKATEBOARDING FASTER AND take fewer spills, if you have a helper, wear proper clothes, and have a safe place to practice.

GET A HELPER

If a fence is the only thing you can use to hold onto while learning to balance, that's okay. But it's more fun, and easier, learning with a friend standing by. The friend can be anyone—skateboarder, or not.

A friend can steady you on the board until you know how to balance yourself. A friend can pull you as you ride on level pavement. Until you learn how to stop properly, a friend can catch your board when you get off.

Champion Laura Thornhill helps a beginner.

Expect to get some laughs. Beginners in anything usually do. However, you will find that other skateboarders are glad to help a beginner.

Most experienced skateboarders say they practiced about two hours a day for two weeks or so, before they felt sure of their balance. For some, it took longer.

If there is absolutely no one to help you, and no fence, use a pair of poles, such as Roller Ski Poles. They look like ski poles, but are specially made for use on pavement.

WHAT TO WEAR

Naturally, you will want to wear clothing that will let your body feel free. At the same time, you want to give your

28

body the protection it needs when you fall. (Chapter 4 explains how you can fall safely.) Even professionals fall. But they wear protective clothing and special gear when they are practicing.

Wear old, loose clothing that covers your knees and elbows. Old jeans or corduroy pants are great. Roll up the legs to make pads for your knees. Wear a top of some thick material such as a heavy sweat shirt. Roll up the sleeves to act as pads for your elbows.

DON'T RIDE BAREFOOT. Feet sweat and make the surface of the skateboard slippery. Not even grip tape will prevent a slippery surface under bare feet. You could slip off when you least expect it.

Wear shoes with nonslip soles. You can't beat sneakers. If your ankles need more strength, wear high sneakers. Professionals always wear nonslip shoes, except in the few tricks where they grip the ends of the board with their toes.

More and more skateboarders today are wearing protective hand gear. And hand protectors are required in downhill racing competitions.

One kind of protector is work gloves with leather palms. You can do the same thing racing skateboarders usually do: stuff two-inch-thick foam rubber into your gloves for added protection.

Another kind of hand protector looks like a thick plastic plate held against the palm by elastic loops. The plates allow you to slide to a stop after falling, rather than stopping you suddenly, as gloves do. With gloves, your hands may stop

Protective gear for the skateboarder.

against the pavement, but your body still moves. Your body can jam its weight against your wrist, and a fracture can result.

To protect knees and elbows, you can buy the kind of pads worn by basketball and volleyball players. Made of knitted cotton with foam rubber pads, they slip on easily over pants legs or jacket sleeves. And they can be stuffed into your pockets when they're not in use.

You can also make pads from men's crew socks. Cut off the feet and roll up the legs. Slip on to protect knees or elbows.

Another important item of protective gear is a helmet. Helmets are always required in downhill racing events, and sometimes in special stunt routines. Professionals wear helmets when they are practicing. You can wear a bicycle helmet.

WHERE TO SKATEBOARD

More skateboard accidents result from poor skating surfaces than from any other cause.

For good skateboarding, you need a wide area so that you don't have to worry about guiding your skateboard while still learning to balance yourself. Also, you need running space to come to a stop without banging into a wall or landing in thorny bushes, or some other unpleasant end. Get into the habit of looking ahead to where your skateboard is taking you!

It's better for beginners if the skateboarding area slopes gently, so you can start off with both feet on the board and coast. Later, when you have learned how to *push-off* without pushing the board out from under yourself, you won't need to coast to get started.

MAKE SURE YOUR AREA DOESN'T SLOPE INTO THE STREET. *DON'T USE A DRIVEWAY WHICH ALSO LEADS INTO THE STREET.*

As a beginner, it is very important that you have the *best* possible skating surface. The area should be smooth and well-paved.

It is also important that the surface be clean. In competitions, the areas are swept with brooms. Even the long down-

An ideal area in which to learn how to skateboard.

hill race courses are swept clean of sand. If officials can use brooms, so can you.

Only a few cities have specially built skateboard parks. And in some cities, it is illegal to skateboard on streets or sidewalks. To learn where skateboarding is legal, check with the parks and recreation department of your city, or with the police. You and your friends may want to set up special skateboarding areas. Get in touch with your local officials who may be willing to work with you.

THE LEARNING SKATEBOARD

It is a good idea to borrow a skateboard before you buy one. That way you can see if you like skateboarding enough to spend money on a board. If you can, try out a few different kinds of boards before you buy. You will be able to tell which kind of skateboard suits you best.

Borrow a smaller board at first, if one is available. A small board is easier to control than a big one when you're learning. (See Chapter 6, Buying A Board For Yourself.) Also, smaller wheels are easier to balance on.

SKATEBOARD INSPECTION

Before setting foot on any skateboard, at any time, check it out for safety.

Here is the 1, 2, 3 Inspection Check List. You should be able to answer "Yes" to every question. One single "No" means the skateboard is *not safe*.

1. INSPECT THE BOARD

Is the board free of cracks?

Is the board free of splinters and rough edges?

Is there a good gripping surface on the deck so that your feet won't slip?

2. INSPECT THE TRUCKS

Is the metal free of cracks in each truck?

Is each truck firmly bolted to the board?

Bolts have a way of working loose. To test, grip the wheels and twist; try to pull the truck from the board. If the trucks do not move, they are firmly bolted.

Are the bushings in good condition? Will they keep the metal parts from touching each other when there is weight and pressure on the board? If they look ragged or chewed up, they are dangerous to ride.

3. INSPECT THE WHEELS

Are the wheels free of cracks?

Do the wheels spin freely without wobbling? To test, brush wheels lightly with the palm of your hand.

Are the bearings free of grease, dirt and rust? If you are using loose bearings, are there sixteen in each wheel?

When you know what to look for, the 1, 2, 3 inspection check takes less than a minute. It could be the most valuable minute you spend in skateboarding.

OTHER CONDITIONS

Never skateboard after dark.

Make sure you can see and be seen.

Avoid wet pavement. Polyurethane wheels get slick when wet. When your wheels are slick, you lose control of your board. (Grease spots cause the same problem.) And water causes bearings to rust unless you clean and dry them immediately. Rust in the wheels can cause a wheel to freeze—stop rolling suddenly. It takes less time to pick up your board and walk around the puddle than it does to dry the bearings.

Never try to do more than you really know. Don't go all out for a trick or ride a hill just because someone else does it. Work up to it.

Now you're ready to learn how to get on and off a skateboard—and ride.

Driver, backing out of driveway, cannot see skateboarder.

CHAPTER 4

How to Ride

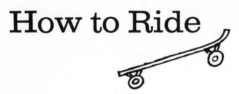

BALANCE IS WHAT SKATEBOARDING IS ALL about. And balance is the first thing a beginning skater has to learn.

Skateboarding requires a different kind of balance from other balance sports, such as skating or bicycling. A skateboard not only rolls, it also wobbles when you step on it.

SITTING ON THE BOARD

To get the feel of the board's movement, sit between the front and back trucks, facing front. Take hold of the board, making sure your fingers are where they won't get pinched. Have your helper give you a gentle push. Coast.

STANDING

Before you step onto the board, ask your helper to take

hold of you at the waist. Grasp the helper's shoulder.

Place your feet on the space between the trucks. If you stand too near either end of the board, the board will tip you off. Also, make sure that your feet are in the middle of the board, not near the edge.

Ask your helper to move you forward slowly. Go a short distance—perhaps 10 feet or so. Jump off. Repeat until you have the feel of it.

Now, have your helper pull you along by one hand as you try to balance yourself (Fig. 1). Continue until you can let go of your helper's hand. Coast.

Fig. 1

GOING IT ALONE

If you have a gentle slope, now you might want to try riding down it alone. Choose a spot part way up, rather than at the top. Ask your helper to steady you until you get both feet on the board. When your helper lets go, bend your knees slightly, and hold your arms out from your sides to balance. Coast. As your balance improves, move your starting point farther up the slope.

The next step is to learn how to get rolling by yourself on level pavement.

THE PUSH-OFF START

1. Place one foot on the center of the board, well back of the front truck (Fig. 2). Bend your knee slightly. Lean forward a bit from the waist.

2. Set your other foot on the pavement near the nose of the board, and push gently against the pavement to go forward (Fig. 3). If you push too hard, you may go too fast, or push the board out from under you.

3. Now, as you lift your pushing foot from the pavement, shift your weight to the other foot. Keep your weight centered over the board at all times.

4. Repeat until it feels natural to you. Push smoothly. Try to develop a rhythm.

Fig. 2

Fig. 3

Fig. 4

5. Now, as you finish a pushing stroke, try placing your pushing foot on the board in front of, or behind, your other foot—whichever is more comfortable for you (Fig. 4).

6. Coast until you need to push again to keep going. Bend your knees slightly so that your body weight is always centered over the board.

RIDING STYLE

The way you stand on your board is your riding style.

Fig. 5   Fig. 6

There are two basic styles: regular foot and goofy-foot.

With regular foot, you ride with the left foot in front (Fig. 5). It's easier for you to turn your body to the right.

Don't let the name goofy-foot turn you off. *Goofy-foot* is the opposite of regular foot. Your right foot is in front, and it's easier to look left (Fig. 6). Some of the best skateboarders are goofy-footed. Use the style that feels comfortable to you.

43

HOW TO STOP

There aren't any brakes on a skateboard, so how do you stop?

If you are going very slowly, one way is to drag your pushing foot against the pavement until you slow your board to a stop. Then, step off the board quickly. Either stop the board with your foot, or pick it up.

If you are going faster, but not too fast, set your pushing

Fig. 7

Fig. 8

foot on the pavement ahead of you, and let your board carry you one step length.

The most frequently used stop is the running step off.

1. Before the board stops rolling, move your pushing foot off and hold it about even with the nose (Fig. 7).

2. Step off with one foot (Fig. 8).

3. Then with your other foot, quickly step off *ahead* of the first foot, as when running (Fig. 9).

4. Keep running until you can slow to a stop (Fig. 10).

Fig. 9

Fig. 10

Fig. 11

OTHER STOPS

When you have learned to ride well, there are other ways to slow down and to stop. One way is the *wheelie* stop. You stop by dragging the tail of your board against the pavement. Keep pressing the tail down with your pushing foot until it really drags (Fig. 11). You will slow to a stop. This works best with wood boards. But it's hard on tails.

Another way to stop or slow down is by making quick right and left curves. Make enough turns to slow, and then come to a stop.

RIGHT AND LEFT TURNS

You've learned to stop without brakes—now how do you steer without a steering wheel? You shift your body weight.

Before stepping onto your skateboard, practice these movements a few times:

1. Place your feet as in riding.
2. Bend your knees slightly.
3. Keep your elbows in toward your waist, your hands loose at your sides.
4. Lean slightly forward from the hips.
5. Keep your shoulders even.

To turn right: Lean from the hips toward your right.

To turn left: Lean from the hips toward your left.

As you make your turns, your *whole* upper body must lean from the hips; do not bend from the waist. And bend your knees more.

Stand before a mirror to see if you are doing it correctly. Then when you're sure you've got it right, go out and practice making turns (Fig. 12).

You might like to set up a practice course. In place of cones, use milk cartons filled with dirt and sealed. Or with chalk, mark Xs on the pavement. Make a long line of markers —either milk cartons or Xs—every four or five feet. Weave right and left between them. As you learn to control your board better, shorten the distance between the markers until they are only about two feet apart. Weaving is a great way to learn body control. And it's fun.

Fig. 12

HOW TO FALL SAFELY

In any of the sports where balance is important, even the experts take spills. But they get up quickly and go on. Champion skateboarders do the same. They know how to fall.

Why fall? The two main causes for spills are losing your balance and losing control of your board. When you feel you are about to lose control, get off your board if it is safe to do so. If you decide to ride it out, crouch low. This lowers your center of gravity so that you have less distance to fall. Also, you have a better chance to get back your control. But riding low to the board increases your speed. If you have not been going very fast, it may not make that much difference. Otherwise, adding even more speed may be a problem. Slow down if you can.

When you know you are going to fall, it is natural for you to tense up. This is the *worst* thing you can do. Gymnasts and judo experts teach us that the key to falling safely is knowing how to relax. Telling yourself "relax" as you're falling, doesn't do it. But you can train yourself to do a judo roll.

Prepare to tumble sideways.

1. Tuck your head down (Fig. 13).

2. Drop one shoulder in the direction you intend to fall (Fig. 13).

3. Keep your elbows close to your body (Fig. 14).

4. Stay as relaxed as you can, and roll off sideways (Fig. 15). Rolling distributes the weight so that no one portion of your body has to take your whole weight (Fig. 16).

Practice tumbling until falling safely becomes a natural reaction. Remember, the object of tumbling is to protect the unpadded parts of your body: head, shoulders, elbows, and

Champion Chris Chaput demonstrates how *not* to fall.

Fig. 13

Fig. 14

Fig. 15

Fig. 16

Fig. 17

ankles. Let the naturally padded parts of your body take the pressures as you roll (Fig. 17). The naturally padded parts are the large muscle areas of your forearms, buttocks, thighs, and calves.

Practice tumbling backward as well as forward so that relaxing and rolling become natural in any fall.

BODY COORDINATION

Skateboarding requires the mind and the body to work together. And that takes practice. And more practice.

52

CHAPTER 5

Tricks, Techniques and Skills

WHEN YOU FEEL SURE OF YOURSELF SKATE-
boarding, you may want to learn to do some tricks.

It is impossible to say which trick will be the easiest
for you to do. For some, the half-circle, or 180°, is the easiest.
For others, the easiest may be a handstand. So, the following
tricks are not listed in the order of increasing difficulty—
although it might work out that way for you.

Some tricks are done starting with the skateboard at rest.
Others require that the board be rolling first. It may surprise
you to discover that it is easier to balance your body on a
moving skateboard than one standing still.

Before trying any tricks, a technique you should know
is weighting. *To weight* means to bear down, to place the
weight of your body on a certain part. For example, to weight

your foot means to press (not stomp) down with all your weight on one foot.

In weighting during tricks, a board with a kicktail has a special advantage. When the tail is weighted—that is, when your foot is pressing down on the tail—that foot is still parallel with the pavement even though the nose of your board is up. However, a kicktail board is not essential for tricks.

TRICKS

180°s (One-Eightys)

You can do either a forward or backward 180°. Using a kicktail makes doing it easier.

Weight your foot on the tail (Fig. 18). As the nose lifts, hold your other foot against it to keep the board in mid-air. With your feet and arms, swing yourself around in a half-circle, or 180° (Fig. 19). You will be facing in the opposite direction from where you started (Fig. 20). The backward 180° is more difficult to do because it's harder to keep your balance when swinging backward.

Fig. 18

Fig. 19

Fig. 20

Endovers

Endovers are like a series of 180°s. Begin by weighting the nose and swinging the tail forward 180° (Fig. 21). Then switch to weighting the tail and swinging the nose forward 180° (Fig. 22). You will be facing first one direction and then the other.

Kick-turns

With both feet across the ends of the board (Fig. 23), weight the tail to move the nose three or four inches to one side (Fig. 24). When the nose hits the pavement, you will roll forward (Fig. 25). Repeat in the opposite direction.

During a planned series of tricks, the constant forward

Fig. 21   Fig. 22

Fig. 23

Fig. 24

Fig. 25

motion of kick-turns allows you to move smoothly from one trick into another without touching the foot to the pavement.

Wheelies

Wheelies are advanced tricks, and are among the most difficult to do. They require lots of practice.

Standard Tail Wheelie

This is easier to do than any of the other wheelies. It is the only wheelie which allows the board to touch the pavement.

While you are rolling, place your riding foot across the tail of the board. Then weight the tail with that foot.

To slow down, use your front foot to let the tail drag. Or, you can just keep rolling. You are riding the tail.

One-Footed Tail Wheelie

This is done by riding forward with one foot on the tail of the board, while the nose is in the air (Fig. 26).

Begin by rolling forward slowly. Move one foot to the tail. Weight the tail. Bend your knee if it helps you to balance. Lift your pushing foot and let it hang free to balance.

Keep rolling. Don't drag the tail.

Two-Footed Tail Wheelie

With your feet side by side and pointed forward, ride the tail of the board with its nose in the air.

58

Fig. 26   Fig. 27

Champion Chynese Smith does a one-footed tail wheelie (right) and a one-footed nose wheelie (left) .

Hold your arms in front of you.

Let your ankles work like hinges to keep the nose up and the tail from dragging the pavement.

One-Footed Nose Wheelie

This trick is done by riding forward on the nose of the board with the tail in the air (Fig. 27).

As you roll forward, place your riding foot on the nose, as close to the end of the board as you can without the foot hanging over. Bend your knee. To help balance yourself, let the other foot hang free, and hold your arms out in front of you.

Roll forward.

Two-Footed Nose Wheelie

While rolling forward, place both feet side by side on the nose, as close to the end of the board as you can without their hanging over (Fig. 28). As the tail lifts, bend your knees, and hold your arms forward to help balance yourself.

Wheelies can be done going backward, but they are more difficult to do. They are also more dangerous because you can't see what you may be running into.

Fig. 28

Champion Mike Dimon does a two-footed nose wheelie.

Hang Ten

Surfers hang ten when they have all ten toes over the front edge of their surfboards. Skateboarders can do the same, *but wear shoes.*

Place both feet side by side with toes over the nose of the board. Roll with all wheels on the pavement. To balance, bend your knees, hold your arms out front, and lean back slightly at the hips.

Hang Five

Hang the toes of the riding foot over the nose of the board (Fig. 29), and bend your knee enough to balance yourself.

The other foot is just behind the front wheels. All wheels are on the pavement.

Use your arms and upper body to balance with.

Fig. 29

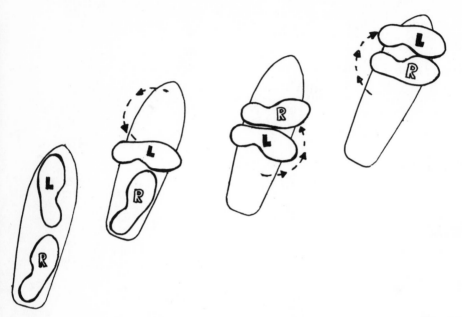

Fig. 30

Walking the Board, or Walking the Dog

Let us suppose you are riding with your left foot forward and your right foot near the tail (Fig. 30).

Bring your left foot back to the center and at right angles with the board. Weight your left foot.

Cross your right foot over your left until it rests on the side of your left foot. Shift your weight onto your right foot.

Bring the left foot from behind the right. Your feet are

now side by side again. They are at right angles with the board.

Take these cross-over steps the length of the board, and reverse to return to your riding position.

Handstands

The rolling motion of the skateboard makes it easier to do a handstand while moving, than to do one on the ground. Even so, practice a few on the grass or gym pad to develop your kick and your arm and wrist strength.

Set the skateboard on the pavement, heading it either to your right or to your left, whichever feels more natural to you.

Grab both ends of the board and roll the board forward, running with it as you do (Fig. 31). Start slowly, then pick

Fig. 31 Champion Chris Chaput prepares to do a handstand.

Fig. 34

up speed. When you get going, kick your legs up over your head (Figs. 32, 33). Curve your body to make turn (Fig. 34).

360°s (Three-Sixtys)

A 360° is a very difficult trick.

Ride with your feet across the board, not pointed forward.

Champion Laura Thornhill begins a Three-sixty.

Fig. 35

Fig. 38

Fig. 39

Fig. 36

Fig. 37

Fig. 40

Place your back foot on the tail (Fig. 35). Look in the direction in which you want to swing, but hold your arms and hands in the opposite direction.

Lean back toward the tail (Fig. 36). As the nose wheels lift, swing your arms in a circle (Fig. 37). If you swing hard enough, this will pull you around in a complete circle (Figs. 38, 39, 40).

Freestyle

Freestyle is a routine or series of tricks, done one after another. As in figure ice skating, freestyling in skateboarding is *your* routine of tricks. You choose the tricks, the order in which you want to do them, and the style you will use going from one trick to the next. The object is to skateboard with a smooth flow of movement, making it all look easy.

In a contest, there is a set limit of time for your act, usually from one to two minutes.

Hot Dogging

Hot dogging is often heard in connection with freestyling. It is another term borrowed from skiing and surfing. In skateboarding, it means to skateboard in an especially exciting manner.

OTHER TECHNIQUES

Curbies

To go up a curb, do a tail wheelie so that the nose of your board lifts above the curb (Fig. 41). Then quickly do a nose wheelie (Fig. 42) so as to lift the tail on to the top of the curb (Fig. 43). This curbie is called "popping a wheelie."

Fig. 41

Fig. 42

Fig. 43

Fig. 44   Fig. 45

To come off a curb, weight your back foot (Fig. 44). Before your board goes over the edge, lift the front wheels (Fig. 44). Bend your knees as you drop (Fig. 45).

If you do too many curbies, you may break or bend your axles.

Flat-Tracking

Once you have learned to do kick-turns, you can flat-track. Flat-tracking is moving along on level stretches without pushing against the pavement to keep going. This skill combines kick-turns with weighting the board in a pumping action.

70

Place one foot across the tail, and your other foot at the center of the board, pointing forward (Fig. 46). Do kickturns until your board starts rolling (Fig. 47). Now twist your back foot around to point forward (Fig. 48). Then bending both legs, weight down sharply on the center of the board to pump (Fig. 48) and let up by straightening your legs a bit. Continue pumping in this way until you reach the speed you can handle. Pump when you need to pick up speed again.

Fig. 46

Fig. 47

Fig. 48

To flat-track easily, you need a board with lots of flexibility or flex. *Flex* means that the board will bend under pressure and return to its original position. This bending and straightening of the board is what gives it forward motion.

Flat-tracking is a skill you must learn if you want to race where there are no hills. If there are low hills, it is fun to see how far up you can flat-track it. If you do much flat-tracking, you want a flex board. (See Chapter 6, Buying A Board For Yourself.)

Slalom

Slalom is a ski term. You can slalom in skateboarding, too. Most skateboard competitions include a downhill slalom event where you weave in and out between cones set in a line. (The spaces between cones are called *gates*.) Slalom is not

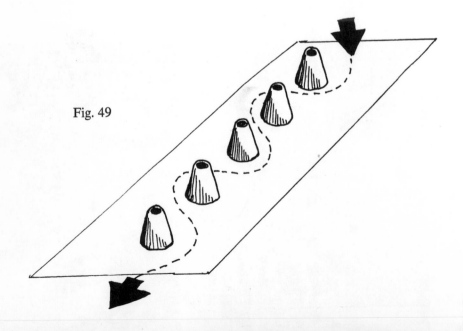

Fig. 49

difficult for beginners. But do wear sneakers, gloves, pads, and a helmet. Slalom only on dry pavement.

There are two slalom course patterns. One pattern is with the cones set in a straight line (Fig. 49). The other is a switchback pattern where the cones make a zigzag pattern downhill (Fig. 50). In a straight line pattern, the shorter the gates are between the cones, the more difficult the course. In the switchback course, the wider apart the cones are, the more difficult the course is. Most courses combine the two patterns.

All slalom courses begin with a starting area of about 15 to 20 feet before the starting line. Only one contestant at a time is allowed on the course, and the time is recorded from starting line to finish. The contestant who completes the course in the shortest time is the winner. Time penalties are made for knocking over any cones.

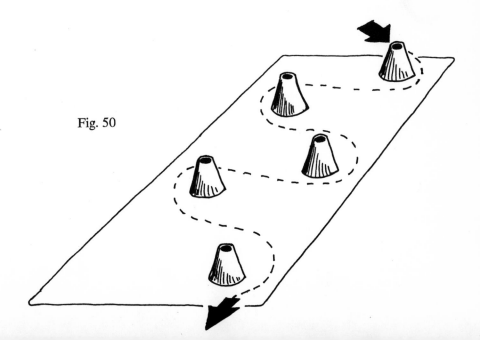

Fig. 50

The diagrams show both patterns, plus a third combination pattern which is the one used by the City of Los Angeles Department of Recreation and Parks (Fig. 51).

For a practice course, use cones without base lips. If

Starting Line

Fig. 51

Repeat pattern once from third cone on. Twenty cones make up the course.

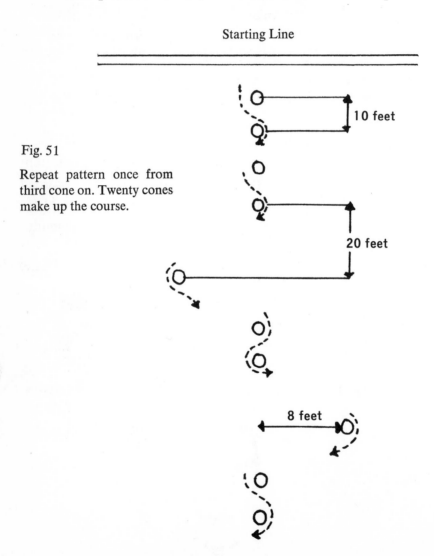

10 feet

20 feet

8 feet

there is an edge on them, trim it off to prevent getting your wheels caught. If you don't have cones, use milk cartons weighted with sand. Seal the tops to prevent spillage when they are knocked over.

But even before you try a full course, practice on a slope—or part-way up a slope—which allows you to make three or four turns without gaining more speed than you can handle.

Begin with a push-off start. In competition, you want to get off to a fast start. So you push to gain as much speed as you can handle, and then you don't push any during the race. After you cross the starting line, reposition your feet so that each foot is across the ends of the board. The object is to control your speed so that you can skate close to the cones without knocking them over.

To keep control of your board, you must make short sharp turns. If you make wide, easy loops, you will gain too much speed and lose control.

As you approach the cone, raise yourself slightly. Then when you're in the turn, bend the knees more and lean back —almost as if you were about to sit down on a chair—and weight your back foot. As you start to come out of the turn, straighten slightly and lean your forward shoulder toward the turn. At the same time, weight your rear foot as if you were trying to push the board to go sideways and downhill.

Seven-year-old Jennifer Dimon leads Chynese Smith and Mike Dimon in a straight-line slalom. Jennifer won a first in slalom competition.

DOWNHILL RACING

Downhill racing is something to look forward to when you know how to control your board while speeding. Heavy skateboards have weight to their advantage. Make sure your board is in tiptop condition. And wide wheels are best.

76

Place your feet in the middle of the board, pointed forward. Crouch into a *tight tuck,* which means placing your body into a position that offers the least wind resistance. Streamlining your body in this way is called *faring.*

Start on short hills with no cross street before your stopping point. Don't try the long hills until you feel you are expert.

COMPETITIONS

Competitions, or skateboard meets, for amateurs are sponsored either by skateboard manufacturers or by a community. When you think you can do as well as other skateboarders in your neighborhood, inquire about entering.

Most competitions require that your equipment pass safety inspection, that you pay a small entry fee which covers accident insurance for you in the competition, and that in the preliminaries, you prove that you are competent.

There are girls' divisions and boys' divisions, as well as divisions by ages—9 and under, 10 to 12, 13 to 16, and over 16 for senior men and senior women. There are freestyle contests for all divisions. Racing events depend upon the location of the meet.

Many of the championship title holders started this way, only a year or two before they won their titles. Watch for demonstrations and competitions held near where you live. You can learn from champions.

CHAPTER 6

Buying a Board
for Yourself

TODAY THERE IS A WIDE VARIETY OF SKATE-
boarding equipment. When you're ready to buy a skateboard,
take the time to get to know the stores that sell and service
them.

WHERE TO BUY

If it is at all possible, deal with sporting goods stores.
They sell replacement parts and do repair service. Some of
them offer free adjustments and wheel cleaning for their customers. These sporting goods stores are more likely to stock
only the brands that are reliable. Also, their clerks are often
skateboarders who can give you good advice because they
have tried out the equipment. A top-quality item will cost
you no more here than at a store which offers no extra services.

As a rule, department stores do not have skateboard repair service even though they may sell good equipment. But watch out for stores which advertise "cut rate" prices. They may be selling cheap skateboards which break easily.

Some of the best skateboarding equipment made can be purchased through the mail. *Skateboarder* magazine carries advertisements of shops and manufacturers who sell in this way. They list items, brand names, prices, and tell you how to order. (*See also* List of Sources And Products.)

FULLY ASSEMBLED SKATEBOARDS

It is easy to be confused by the names. A fully assembled

skateboard, with its three components (parts) may be made by the same manufacturer. But sometimes one company makes the boards, another the trucks, and still another the wheels. The combination may be top quality, or it may not.

Buying a fully assembled skateboard costs less than if you were to buy the components separately and assemble them yourself. The important thing is to look for quality— good quality board, good trucks and wheels.

STIFF BOARD OR FLEX BOARD?

When you are talking with clerks and other skateboarders, there are two terms you will hear again and again —*stiff* and *flex,* or flexible. A stiff board will bend very little, if at all. The flexible board will bend and return to its original position.

Boards have different degrees of flexibility. It depends upon the material, its thickness, and the length of the board. A board's flexibility can also be changed by either tightening the trucks or loosening them.

It is easier to learn to balance yourself on a stiff board. This kind of board has little up-and-down give. The most common stiff board is one made of wood with the trucks tightened.

How much flex do you want?

You should have a flex of ¼ inch to ½ inch when you stand on the board. There should be a ½- to 1-inch flex when

you bounce on it without *bottoming out,* that is, without the board's middle hitting the pavement.

Both stiff and flex boards are made either of hardwood or aluminum, masonite, fiberglass, "lexan," or other plastics. One very good flex board is a combination of *laminated* layers of wood and fiberglass (laminated means layers of material glued together under pressure). Any board that is laminated is a stronger board. It is less likely to crack down the center or break in the middle.

Both stiff and flex boards can have *camber,* which means

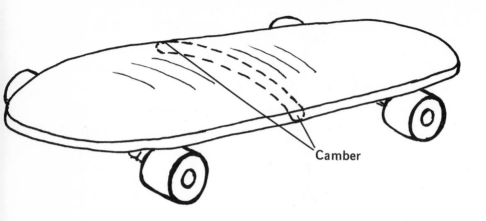

Camber

Fig. 51A

that the board curves up toward the top and center of the board so that the center appears thicker than the edges (Fig. 51A). Camber on a board allows the board to flex more without bottoming out.

The opposite of camber is the *dished* top. As you might guess, the top is slightly scooped out, just like a dish. The dished top gives something to brace your feet against, helping you keep from sliding off.

WOOD BOARDS

These offer a certain natural beauty. They may get bad scratches and gouges. Skateboarders call a scarred board *dinged up,* a surfing term. But wood boards can be resanded and refinished to look almost new again.

82

Ash, birch, hickory, oak, mahogany, and walnut are the woods used. Ash is the most popular because it is both light in weight and strong, and is also the cheapest. It will bend under stress without breaking. Soft woods, such as pine, are not used because they crack easily.

Another advantage to a wood board is that it is easier to change the placement of the trucks than on a molded board of manmade materials. You may want to use better trucks on your skateboard some day. (See Chapter 8.) Or, your style of riding will change, and you will want different trucks and wheels.

Wood also gives a smoother ride. It absorbs more of the vibration of riding than other materials do.

PLASTIC BOARDS

Some of the best skateboards are made of plastic. Fiberglass, "lexan," and polyurethane are a few of the plastics used. They come in many colors and combinations of colors, and some are transparent with no color at all.

One advantage of the plastic board is that it is lighter than wood or metal. Being lightweight, it is easier to handle when you are learning or for doing tricks.

A disadvantage is that when they get battered, there isn't much you can do about it. You've got to buy a new one.

Before buying a plastic board, check for cracks. These show up as white streaks part way along the length of the

board. Also make sure that the trucks are bolted on all the way through the board with the bolt heads showing flush (even) with the deck. If they are not, the bolts can pull through, resulting in a bad accident.

ALUMINUM BOARDS

The advantages of aluminum boards is that they are

strong and don't wear out. But, like plastic, if they get scarred, there is nothing you can do about it. The major disadvantage, though, is that they make your feet and ankles more tired when you do lots of skateboarding. It is like standing on metal floors for hours.

QUALITY IN TRUCKS

The manufacturers of trucks offer many varieties. If you ever want to make changes to your skateboard or build your own, you can choose the trucks you want and buy them separately.

Good trucks are made of case-hardened steel (a special treatment to make the outer surface extra hard), or of an aircraft-quality aluminum. Cheaper trucks are made of junk metal (reshaped, used metal). These can easily crack and break. The especially low-priced, fully assembled skateboard often has these cheap trucks. If you are small and lightweight, they might hold up until you learn to balance—but that's about all.

Look at the bushings on the trucks. Are there two thick ones made of rubber or vinyl? Either material is good. Vinyl (a type of plastic) is stiff until broken in, but it lasts longer than the rubber bushings.

Is there a pad between the board and the base plate? This pad is a shock absorber. It is sometimes called a *spacer*. Such a pad will give you a smoother ride. However, while you are still learning and getting your balance, you might want to remove the pad to lower your center of gravity. Later, if you start doing slaloms or flat-tracks, you can put the spacer back on again. It prevents your board from bottoming out or binding against the wheels on sharp turns.

Metal base plates are the only reliable ones. Those made of plastic crack.

Skip the trucks that have springs instead of bushings, for now. They are only for experts who are going in for speed.

Check the axles. These, too, should be of case-hardened steel or high-quality aluminum. Axles vary in widths from 2 inches to 4½ inches between the wheels. Try to get a truck with axles about 2 inches or 2½ inches wide.

WHEELS

Wheels have two measurements—diameter and tread, or width. The diameter makes the difference between a low or a high center of gravity. When learning, you want a low center of gravity. Like heels on shoes, even a quarter of an inch makes a big difference. Wheels with a larger diameter travel faster but, at first, you don't want to go very fast.

The wider the tread is on a wheel, the less chance there is to skid. But the wider they are, the harder they are to turn.

A good standard size wheel has a diameter of 1½ inches to 1⅞ inches with a two-inch tread.

BEARINGS

Skateboard wheels turn on ball bearings. At first, wheels were made with a bearing cone to hold in loose bearings. Now wheels are made with sealed bearings.

Sealed bearings offer many advantages. The bearings do not fall out, and they stay clean, longer. (But they will rust if they get wet.) They roll quietly.

THE BOARD FOR YOU

Start with a skateboard that is sturdy, but not too heavy. Choose one about 20 to 24 inches long (shorter ones for shorter skaters), 5 to 7 inches wide. Get standard size wheels —$1\frac{7}{8}$ inches in diameter with two-inch tread. Insist on standard double-action adjustable trucks with axle width of 2 to $2\frac{1}{2}$ inches between the wheels.

Decide whether you want a flat board or one with a kicktail. If you plan to do tricks, a kicktail gives you a definite advantage. The double-kick is too awkward to use in the beginning.

Right now there are 50 or more models to choose from. New materials and new designs keep coming on the market every day.

CHAPTER 7

Taking Care of and Upgrading Your Equipment

AFTER EACH DAY OF SKATEBOARDING, GIVE your equipment a thorough cleaning and overhauling. Use the 1, 2, 3 Inspection Check List (Chapter 3) as a reminder.

BESIDES A SKATEBOARD

When you buy your skateboard, also buy some grip tape. Grip tape has a rough surface and a peel-off backing that is self-adhesive. The tape comes in various widths and is sold by the foot. The pattern of grip tape is not for beauty, but to keep you from slipping off the board. Use a wide strip down the center. Or apply to the deck where you think it will help the most.

A skateboard tool is something you will want to have.

Two kinds of skateboard tools.

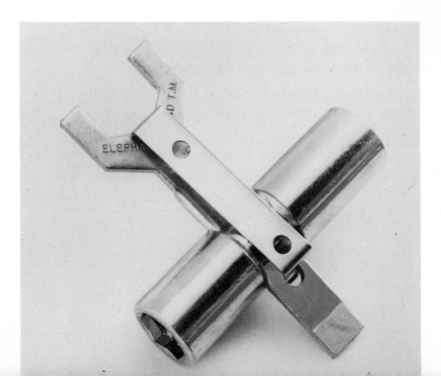

It is a combination of small tools—all in one—that has many purposes, such as to tighten the wheel nuts of loose bearing wheels and to tighten or loosen the trucks. Get the combination of wrench sizes that will best suit your skateboard. You can carry the tool with you by taping it with electrician's black tape to the underside of your board. There are gadgets for holding the tool on the board, but, so far, none of them works too well. It's not a good idea to carry the tool in your pocket, because it could hurt you if you fell on that side.

Another necessity is a lubricant. The kind depends on what type of bearings your wheels have.

LUBRICATING WHEEL BEARINGS

If your wheels have loose bearings, you want a dry lubricant. Get a graphite powder or a silicone powder. Each comes in a can. There is also a special lubricant ("Super Skate Spray") in an aerosol can which is very good.

Never use grease, oil, or WD-40 oil lubricant on loose bearings. They attract dirt and sand.

Clean by applying some of the lubricant on each side of the wheel. After using graphite or silicone powder, blow out with an air hose.

Wheels with sealed bearings have seals on both sides to keep the lubricant in and the dirt out (Fig. 52). However, the lubricant will wear out, despite some claims of a "lifetime" lubrication. Add lubricant, such as "moly-grease"

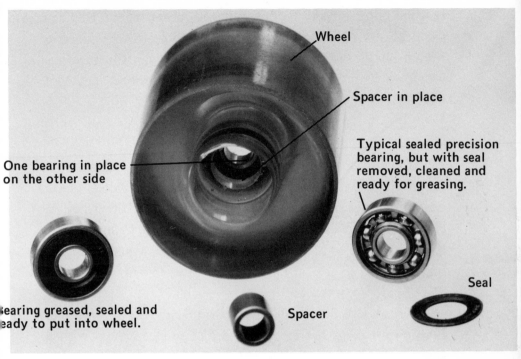

Fig. 52 The parts of a wheel with sealed precision bearings.

(molybdenum disulfide) and you really will have a lifetime lubricant.

To add the lubricant, remove the bearing cones from the wheels. Carefully lift the seals off with your fingernails, and rub moly-grease into each side. You are forcing out the original lubricant and replacing it with a better one. Replace the seals. Put the cone back into the wheels. If you have ridden on the wheels before relubricating, dip the bearings into a solvent to clean first. Proceed as described. (Do not use WD-40.)

SURFACE CARE

If your board gets nicks in it after riding, smooth the rough edges with sandpaper. If your board is wood, put a coat of varnish on the raw wood. Make sure the wood is clean. Use a cheap varnish brush and let dry thoroughly. Exposed wood gets dirty and water logged when it is not sealed with a final coat or varnish. Water logging will cause your board to rot.

To smooth the rough edges of a plastic board, use a file. Plastic dust clogs the teeth of the file, so clean them with a stiff brush as you work.

"TUNING" YOUR BOARD

To *tune* your board means to adjust the wheels and trucks to the kind of riding you wish to do. If you know how to use wrenches and screwdrivers, you probably can make the adjustments yourself. But if you run into difficulty, don't hesitate to ask the clerk where you bought your board or some other adult for help.

To Tune Wheels

Wheels with loose bearings may get to rolling so fast that they wobble. This happens when the bearing cones have loosened. Use the cone end of the skateboard tool, or a socket wrench, to tighten the bearing cone of each wheel. When the nut is quite snug, bring your wrench back a half turn, loosening the cone until the wheel spins again freely and without wobble.

Wheels with sealed bearings need no adjustment. They are held on with a locknut. They roll freely and without wobble.

To Tune Trucks

At first, you want a stiff board to give you stability. Tighten the trucks so that there is little play in the action of the board. You don't want the board to wobble too much when you're learning to balance yourself. Even after you are experienced, you may find that you still prefer a stiff board. Many expert skateboarders do.

To tighten your trucks means to take out as much of the cushioning effect from the bushings as is possible.

Begin by locating the locknut on the action bolt. It is between the base plate and the retainer washer under the action bushing (Fig. 53).

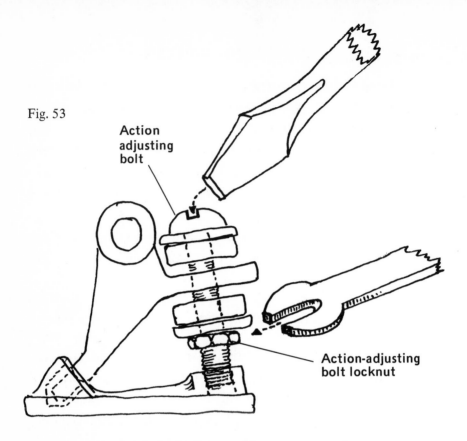

Fig. 53

Action adjusting bolt

Action-adjusting bolt locknut

Loosen the bolt locknut with your wrench.

Screw the action bolt farther into the base plate. Screw in clockwise.

Now, tighten the bolt locknut, holding the action bolt in place, until the locknut is as tight as you can make it. The LOCKNUT MUST BE TIGHT, or it will work loose, and you may strip the threads in the base or off the action bolt.

REPLACING WHEELS

When wheels wear out or you want to use different wheels, they can be replaced. It is not difficult to mount wheels with sealed precision bearings.

Remove the nuts and washers that are on the axle. Slide old wheel off and replace with new wheel.

Secure with a self-locking nut. These locknuts have a nylon locking insert.

Tighten with wrench.

REPLACING AXLES

Axles will break, and bend. (Doing curbies is hard on axles.) When axles are damaged, they must be replaced. Make sure you get a replacement that will fit into the truck you are using. Some axles are $5/16$ of an inch in diameter, and others are $9/32$ of an inch. Lengths run from 4½ inches to 9 inches.

To replace an axle, you must have a vise to hold the truck while you work out the axle. If you don't have a vise, check with your friends and neighbors. They might let you do your repair work at their workbench, since the vise you use must be fastened solidly. You may also need the help of an adult, because the task requires a strong arm.

First, remove the locknuts, wheels, nuts, and washers. Open the vise about ¼ of an inch. Clamp in the axle.

On the axle, there is a small, raised ridge or strip about ⅜ of an inch long called a "knurl." You cannot see it until the axle is out, because it is hidden by the axle-carrying tube. The knurl is to keep the axle from slipping. The knurled end must be removed first. You won't know which end has the knurl until you unscrew the axle. If your axle is bent at this end, you must first straighten it by bending or by pounding it straight.

With the axle clamped into the vise, grasp the truck and turn counterclockwise to unscrew. If the axle won't budge, remove and clamp in the other end and unscrew. DO NOT TRY TO POUND OUT AN AXLE until you have tried unscrewing it. Pounding it out may strip the threads inside the carrying tube, and your truck is ruined. But if all else fails, use a center punch. Place the truck in the vise with the axle pointed up; the end with the knurl, down. Place the end of the punch onto the end of the axle, and tap the top of the punch sharply with a hammer. You may be lucky and have the axle fall out without damaging the inside threads.

When the old axle is out, replace with a new one. Slide knurl-free end into the same side from which you took out the old axle.

Clean the nuts and washers in solvent before putting back on.

REPLACING TRUCKS

Make sure that you have base plates that the trucks can be fitted into. (Not all trucks fit all base plates.) You may have to drill new holes in order to change base plates. (See the instructions and photographs in Chapter 8.)

How to Build Your Own Skateboard

GOOD-QUALITY SKATEBOARDS CAN BE BUILT AT home or as a project in your woodshop class.

You will need hand tools and experience using them. If you don't have all of the tools, ask your friends' families and your neighbors. You probably will need some adult help, too. (Usually where tools are, there is an adult who can show you how to use them.) DO NOT USE POWER TOOLS UNLESS YOU HAVE ADULT SUPERVISION ALL OF THE TIME.

If you can get a good piece of ½-inch wood—ash, hickory, oak, mahogany, walnut—you can save several dollars. (Never use a soft wood such as pine. It cracks and breaks easily.) You can make a better looking board, too. And you can add your own choice of trucks and wheels.

Chris Chaput, world champion skateboarder, makes

Fig. 54

many of the boards he uses. Some of his designs have become the models for new boards now on the market.

SHAPE AND SIZE

If you see a board shape that you like (Fig. 54), trace the outline onto heavy wrapping paper and transfer it to the board. Or you can draw directly on the wood. Use a hand saw to shape the sides. DO NOT SHAPE THE NOSE OR TAIL. In the next step, you will have to find the center of your board, and it is easier to do so before you cut it to shape.

99

Fig. 55

Using a ruler, yardstick, or T-square, divide the width of your board in half by drawing a line down the center from nose to tail (Fig. 55). This will be the guide line for centering the base plates for the trucks.

To cut your board to shape, use a hand saw, such as a coping saw or a scroll saw. If you use motor driven saws—jig, band, or saber saws—do so only with adult supervision.

Round the edges with a wood file and sandpaper. If you use a power tool, a router is required. It is important that the edges of your board are rounded. Sharp edges can splinter or cut. Also, rounded edges give a finished, stream-lined appearance.

Using the center guide line, set the base plates about

100

3 or 4 inches from each end of the board (Fig. 56). A base plate has a front and back. The plate must be placed so that when the truck and wheels are installed, both nose and tail wheels will be nearer the ends of the board than toward the inside.

The base plate in the photographs has only three holes. Using it as an example, center the single hole on the line down the middle of the board. Mark the position through the base plate hole with a sharp pointed pencil or a nail point. Repeat for the plate at the other end of the board. Don't worry about the other two holes now.

If your base plate has more than three holes, find the center of the base plate and center it on the line down the middle of the board. Make a mark through the bolt hole closest to you.

Fig. 56

Drill each of the holes you have marked all the way through the board with a hand drill or a brace and bit. Use a drill bit which is slightly smaller than the screws for the base plate.

Bolt the base plates loosely in that one spot to anchor them temporarily.

Place a yardstick up to the edge of the base plates, forcing them to straighten on the board (Fig. 57). Mark the places for the remaining bolt holes.

Remove the base plates while you drill the remaining bolt holes. With a drill, countersink all the bolt holes on the top side of the deck so that when the base plates are bolted

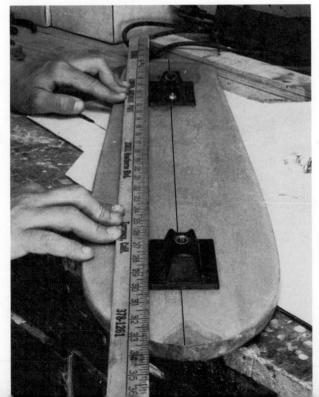

Fig. 57

on, the bolt heads are flush with the surface, not sticking up (Fig. 58). To countersink, use a drill bit the same diameter as the bolt heads.

Before you go further, it is time to sandpaper and paint your board with a good coat of varnish or shellac. (Remove base plate first.) When it is thoroughly dry, continue.

If you are using a base plate pad (also called a shock absorber or spacer), fit it against the bottom of the base plate, and bolt them on from the deck side until the base plate is on as tight as possible. Use #8-32 flathead bolts about ¼ inch longer than needed to go through the board, base plate, and pad (Fig. 58A). Use self-locking nuts (Fig. 59) or

Fig. 58   Fig. 58A

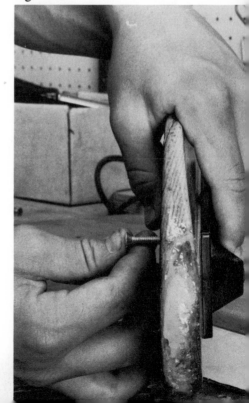

Fig. 59

apply a bolt-tightening solution, so as to be sure that the bolts will not work loose from vibration when riding. Always check bolts before riding.

INSTALLING THE TRUCKS

To install the trucks into the base plates (Fig. 60), use an open-end wrench or a screwdriver. Screw the action bolt nut until there is approximately ½ inch of bolt showing (Fig. 61). Use your thumb to guide the action bolt into its hole

Fig. 60

A double-action adjustable truck with one wheel off. Except for the wheel and the base plate, all the parts shown are considered a part of the truck. All the parts are replaceable. You don't have to buy a whole new truck if you want to replace worn-out bushings or a damaged axle.

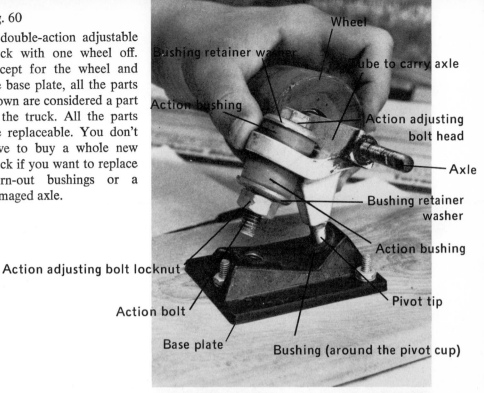

Wheel

Bushing retainer washer

Tube to carry axle

Action bushing

Action adjusting bolt head

Axle

Bushing retainer washer

Action bushing

Action adjusting bolt locknut

Pivot tip

Action bolt

Base plate

Bushing (around the pivot cup)

Fig. 61

in the base plate. Be careful on the first two or three turns that you are not stripping the threads. Do not force the bolt in. Use only light pressure until you know it is going in correctly (Fig. 62). If it doesn't screw in easily, start over. If you cross the threads, you have ruined your base plate. Five or 6

Fig. 62

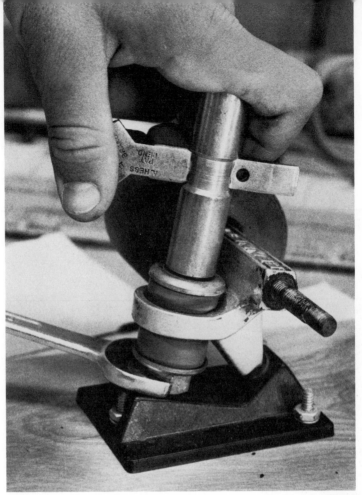

Fig. 63

turns with a socket wrench or skateboard tool will tighten trucks for normal riding (Fig. 63).

When purchasing a truck, the axle is included. You can also buy axles by themselves.

Fig. 64

PLACING THE WHEELS

The photo shows two sealed bearings and the spacer on the axle without the wheel (Fig. 64).

It is a good idea to grease the bearings of new wheels with moly-grease. It comes either in a grease base or as a dry powder. Force the lubricant into the new bearings. (See Chapter 7.)

Put one bearing into the wheel with the seal facing out, unless it is a double seal—then it doesn't matter. Drop the

108

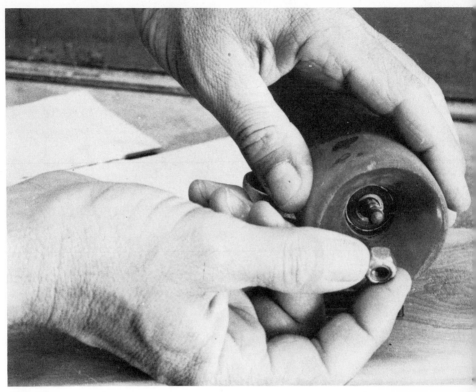

Fig. 65

little spacer in—this separates the bearings—otherwise the
bearing will crush the shoulder at the center of the wheel.
Put the next bearing on with the seal facing out. Press the
bearings in tightly and slip the assembled wheel onto the
axle tightly.

Slip the locknuts onto the axles (Fig. 65). Tighten with
a socket, or cone wrench, until the wheels spin freely, but not

loosely (Fig. 66). Experiment until you learn how tight you want your wheels. All four should spin at about the same speed. (Check Chapter 7 for further description.)

Apply grip tape as described in Chapter 7.

And your very own skateboard is ready to test.

To replace base plates, trucks or wheels, follow the same procedures after removing the old parts.

Fig. 66

CHAPTER 9

Skateboarding and Safety

WHETHER SKATEBOARDING CONTINUES REALLY depends upon its safety record.

FOR THE RECORD

Fortunately, skateboarding in the 1970s proved to be as safe as any other sport—and safer than most—according to the U.S. Consumer Product Safety Commission (CPSC).

But like any sport, skateboarding is dangerous if the rules for safety are not followed. As the number of skateboarders increases, there are bound to be more accidents. Careless skateboarders could ruin the sport for everyone. Some towns have already banned skateboarding because they are afraid of having a repetition of the 1960s.

POLICE PROGRAMS

Some cities, like Santa Monica, California, have begun programs to promote skateboard safety. Their police department, in cooperation with their parks department and schools, sponsors a skateboard inspection. Skateboarders are invited to bring their skateboards to a school where a police officer checks them. If the skateboard passes the safety inspection, the owner then demonstrates skills, making quick stops, right and left turns, and slaloms. Those who pass both equipment and performance tests earn a sticker for the underside of their skateboard. The Safe Skater Sticker is good for a free hamburger.

The attitude of the police was expressed by Officer Dick Barry. "I think the main thing that we can teach youngsters is common courtesy when skateboarding on the sidewalk. If someone is walking toward you, just stop your skateboard, let them pass by. Don't knock them over. As far as accidents are concerned, it's just knowing your limitations . . . not trying something you're not capable of doing yet. It's like learning to drive or anything else. You have to go one step at a time."

FROM THE CHAMPIONS

You can do your part in keeping the accident rate down. The following rules were gathered from some of the national skateboard champions: Robin Alaway, Chris Chaput, Mike

Left to right: Champions Robin Alaway, Gary Kocot and Desirée Von Essen.

Dimon, Skitch Hitchcock, Russ Howell, Bruce Logan, Ed Nadaline, Ty Page, Laura Thornhill, and Desirée Von Essen.

> Skateboard where it is legal.
> Never skateboard at night or on wet pavement.
> Be sure you can see where you are going, and make sure others can see you.
> Wear shoes with nonskid soles (sneakers).

Wear protective clothing and special gear when attempting difficult tricks and when racing.

Match your tricks to your skill.

Check your skateboard regularly, and keep it in good condition.

Think safety at all times.

GOVERNMENT

Most of the skateboarding equipment on the market today is good—very good. When it is not, the CPSC has the power to stop its manufacture. If you have any complaints, send the details to the U.S. Consumer Product Safety Commission, Washington, D.C., 20207. Or, you can call the commission from anywhere in the continental United States, toll free. Simply dial: 800-638-2666. In Maryland, call 800-492-2937.

CHAPTER 10

The Future of
Skateboarding

CITY ACTION

When skateboarding was reborn, there were still memories of past accidents. One of the cities that did not want skateboarders on their streets was Ventura, California. So, they banned skateboarding.

But skateboarders got together and petitioned the city council to reconsider. They spoke before the council, and convinced them that skateboarding could be a fine outdoor sport if it had a proper place. Their arguments were so convincing that the council reversed its decision. The city set aside a few little-used streets for skateboarding. They went a step further and built a small skateboard park on undeveloped city land. It was the first community skateboard park ever to be built.

Slalom event in 1976 competition at Ventura, California.

In 1974, Ventura held a skateboard meet. The event was such a success that they made it an annual affair, and welcomed skateboarders from everywhere. Thousands of spectators saw over three hundred competitors in the 1976 meet. Before the two-day meet was over, plans were being made for a bigger and better meet the next year.

116

DOWN UNDER

On the other side of the world from Ventura, there is another community skateboard park in Albany, Australia. Here, again, skateboarders proved that skateboarding could be a fine sport if it had the proper setting. They proposed that a park be built on some unused land.

The town has a history of supporting their youths' recreation programs. They donated land for a skateboard park. High school skateboarders immediately began a series of fundraising events to get the money for the construction work. Pleased by the young peoples' efforts, civic organizations contributed money to the project.

On opening day of the park, 1200 residents of Albany, Australia, turned out for the event.

In the summer of 1976, the City of Los Angeles began a program of city park skateboard competitions. Plans are under consideration for skateboard parks also.

COMMERCIAL PARKS

The first commercial skateboard park (admission is charged) was built in Chiba, Japan, a small town about 30 miles from Tokyo. It is so popular that it is being enlarged.

Other commercial parks have been built in Daytona Beach and Cocoa, Florida; Carlsbad, California; and Corpus Christi, Texas. Plans are on the drawing boards for many more parks all over the world.

The skateboard park in Carlsbad, California, shortly after it opened in the summer of 1976. The park features concrete dips, banks and modified bowls for skateboarding.

COMPETITIONS

San Diego, California, near the birthplace of skateboarding, was the home for the first world championship competitions. Nearby Del Mar held the first competitions for national championships.

People in other parts of the country heard about the feats skateboarders were able to perform, and they wanted to see for themselves. Skateboarders who held championship titles were invited to compete with each other before a paying audience. The Nassau Invitational Competition on Long Island, New York, in the summer of 1976 was one such event. And skateboarding proved to be an exciting spectator sport.

Anyone can sponsor a competition—an organization, a city, a manufacturer. The manufacturers of skateboarding equipment sponsor them because it is a good way to advertise their products. They also sponsor demonstrations given by champions who use their products to show what can be done on their equipment.

One large company sponsored a team of four skateboarders who toured the United States, giving skill and safety demonstrations.

All of this activity creates more interest in skateboarding. The one threat to its growth is the lack of safe areas for beginners and for pleasure skateboarding. As Jack Dimon says, "The major cause of accidents is from skateboarding on surfaces not designed for skateboarding. We need skateboard parks just as we need bike paths, basketball courts and tennis courts."

Skateboarding's future? Definite. Perhaps it will even go on to be an olympic event some day.

LIST OF TOOLS AND MATERIALS

Tools should be used with adult supervision or by people with experience. You will need the following:

HAND TOOLS

Yardstick or T-Square
Hand saw (for cutting straight lines)
Coping saw or scroll saw (for cutting curves)
Hand drill (the kind you hold with one hand and turn wheel with the
    other), or a brace and bit (a boring tool)
Two drill bits (one should be the same size as the screws for the base
    plate, or slightly smaller; and one should be the same size as the
    screw heads)
Wood file
Screwdriver
Socket, cone, or ratchet wrench
Open-end wrench, $\frac{1}{2}$-inch or $\frac{9}{16}$-inch
Or, a skateboard tool in place of the above three tools
Sandpaper
Small (two-inch) paint brush

POWER TOOLS

Band saw, or saber saw (for cutting straight lines)
Jig saw (for cutting curves)
Router (for rounding edges)
Drill with 2 drill bits

MATERIALS

$\frac{1}{2}$-inch hardwood; length depends on size of skateboard wanted
Varnish or shellac
2 complete skateboard trucks (axles are a part of complete trucks)
4 complete polyurethane wheels
2 or 3 feet of grip tape one inch wide, or other size, depending on
    pattern

LIST OF SOURCES AND PRODUCTS

Magazine:

> *Skateboarder.* Subscriptions: 6 issues per year $6.00 (foreign $7.00), P.O. Box 1028, Dana Point, Ca. 92629.

Manufacturers' Organizations (for skateboarders):

> Hang Ten, 724 N. Poinsettia, Santa Ana, Ca. 92702.
>
> R.A.C.O. Mfg., Inc., 12436 East Putnam, Whittier, Ca. 90602.

National Organizations:

> Co/Mark, Jack Dimon, Skateboard Consultants, 4600 Campus Drive, Newport Beach, Ca. 92660.
>
> Florida Skateboard Association, 106 Victoria, Merritt Island, Fla. 32952.
>
> Pro/Am Skateboard Racing Association, P.O. Box 632, Dana Point, Ca. 92629.
>
> New York Skateboard Association, John Cowalenko, c/o East Coast Promotions, P.O. Box 64, Bellport, N.Y. 11713.
>
> Skateboard Racing Association, 274 Grandview, Laguna Beach, Ca. 92651.

Shops (A few of the shops which handle retail mail orders):

In California:

> General Skateboard Products, 15106 Westate Street, Westminster, 92683. (Skateboard tool and other products.)

Kanoa Surf, 706 Deep Valley Drive, Rolling Hills Estates, 90274 (Handles domestic and foreign orders.)

Skateboard City, 3925-5th Ave., San Diego, 92101.

Steve's South Bay Sporting Goods, 2577 Pacific Coast Highway, Torrance, 90505.

Super Wrench, P.O. Box 163, Huntington Beach, 92648.

In Florida:

Fox Surf Shop, Box 626, 317-C Ocean Ave. (AIA), Melbourne, 32951.

Roller Sports, Inc., 1855 Cassat Ave., Jacksonville, 32210.

In Maryland:

Bethesda Surf Shop, 4931 Cordell Ave., Bethesda, 20014.

In Massachusetts:

Super Wrench, P.O. Box 99, Wilmington, 01887 (Skateboard tool only).

In New Jersey:

Kona Skateboards, Inc. 420 W. Cedar Ave., Wildwood, 08260.

In Texas:

Dockside Shop, 315 Beach St., Port Aransas, 78373.

Skate and Surf Shop, 1817-61st. St., Galveston, 77550.

PRODUCTS

(The following are a few of the brand-name products experienced skateboarders find dependable for all-around recreational skateboarding and freestyling. This list is not intended as a complete list of dependable products.)

BOARDS (Blanks only; 24 or 25-inch lengths with kicktail)

Bahne (comes in wood or fiberglass)
Gordon and Smith (wood or fiberglass laminations) G & S
    Fibreflex
Hang Ten
Logan Earth Ski (wood)

TRUCKS (2 per blank)

Bennett Hijacker
Sure Grip
Tracker Truck
X-Caliber

WHEELS (4 per blank)

O.J.'s (sealed bearings)
Road Rider #2 (sealed bearings)
R. S. Stoker (Roller Sports) (loose bearings)

Glossary

base plate—metal bolted to board to hold the truck.

base plate spacer—shock absorber, or pad, between the board and the base plate.

blank—manufacturer's term for board, or top part of skateboard.

board—top part of skateboard.

bottoming out—bottom of board touches pavement.

bushing—a pad used as a shock absorber.

camber—curve on surface.

chassis—the board of a skateboard.

components—parts.

cone—an object made of rubber or plastic shaped like an upside-down icecream cone.

curbie—technique of going on to and off of curbing and steps.

deck—top surface of board.

dinged up—a skateboard that is scarred with scratches and gouges.

dished—a dip in the surface; the opposite of camber.

double-kick—a board which curves up at both ends.

endovers—a series of one-eightys.

faring—offering least resistance to wind.

flat-tracking—skateboarding on level stretches without pushing against the pavement to keep going.

flex—short for flexible; a board with flexibility.

free jump—a jump over a hurdle to land again on the rolling board on the other side.

freestyle—an individual's style.

freestyling—a routine of tricks.

gate—the space between markers, or cones, through which the skateboarder must pass in a slalom race. The term means the same in ski slalom racing.

goofy-foot—a style of riding with left foot in front of right.

grip tape—self-adhesive, nonskid tape.

hang five—a trick in which toes of one foot hang over front edge of the board.

hang ten—a trick in which toes of both feet hang over front edge of the board.

hot dogging—a flashy style of skateboarding.

kick—a shortened term for other words involving "kick."

kick-out—technique for getting off skateboard.

kick-turn—technique of making a quick turn.

kicktail—curved up end of board.

king pin spacer—a shock absorber; bushing.

nose—front of the board.

nose wheelie—trick of riding on front wheels only.

one-eighty—swinging around in a half-circle.

pad—bushing; shock absorber, as between the board and base plate.

polyurethane—a plastic used in making wheels, boards, and other products.

push-off—technique of moving a skateboard from starting position.

rails—the rounded sides of the board.

riding—having the weight of your whole body on the moving skateboard, whether it is with one foot or two.

shock absorber—pad; bushing; cushion made of rubber or vinyl.

shocks—shortened term for shock absorber.

skateboard—a board with skate wheels attached.

slalom—skiing term used in skateboarding to mean a zigzag course laid out between cones.

spacer—pad or bushing between base plate and the board.

speed wobbles—wheels running loosely during speeding.

stiff—a type of skateboard which has little flexibility.

tail—rear end of board.

three-sixty—swinging around in a full circle.

tight tuck. *See* faring.

toe tap—a kick-turn.

traction—moving ability with the least slippage; resistance to slipping and sliding.

truck—metal axle assembly.

tuning—to adjust the wheels and trucks to your kind of riding.

urethane—shortened term for polyurethane, used by skateboarders.

walking the board—cross-over steps the length of the board.

wheelie—trick involving riding only on nose or tail wheels.

weight—to press down; concentrate your body weight on to one spot.

wipe-out—surfing term, meaning to lose balance and fall during fast skateboarding.